W9-DHO-027

CONTEMPORARY MUSICIANS
AND THEIR MUSIC™

Lifehouse

Rich Juzwiak

The Rosen Publishing Group, Inc., New York

Published in 2007 by The Rosen Publishing Group, Inc.
29 East 21st Street, New York, NY 10010

First Edition

Library of Congress Cataloging-in-Publication Data

Juzwiak, Rich.
Lifehouse/by Rich Juzwiak.
    p. cm.—(Contemporary musicians and their music)
Includes bibliographical references and discography.
ISBN 1-4042-0710-4 (library binding)
1. Lifehouse (Musical group)—Juvenile literature. 2. Rock musicians—United States—Biography—Juvenile literature. I. Title. II. Series.
ML3930.L455J89 2006
782.42166092'2—dc22

                                                                    2005037509

Manufactured in Malaysia

On the cover: Rick Woolstenhulme, Jason Wade, and Bryce Soderberg *(from left)* of Lifehouse arrive at the Radio Music Awards in Las Vegas, Nevada, in 2005.

Contents

Introduction

Lifehouse is onstage, the band members' instruments are plugged in, and yet you can barely hear them. It isn't because the band is playing too quietly. It isn't a matter of faulty wiring or a broken sound system. It's because the audience is so loud, singing the band's song with such force, that the concert venue's speakers come close to giving out. The time is early 2001, and the place is a small club in South Carolina. The song that has everyone in the room going crazy is "Hanging by a Moment." The rest of the country would soon follow suit.

Rick, Jason, and Bryce *(from left)* perform in Atlanta, Georgia, in 2005.

4

This was a moment that was repeated all year long. "Hanging by a Moment" would play on the radio more times than any other song in 2001. It was a multiformat success that jumped from modern-rock stations to Top 40 stations to adult contemporary radio. That first brush with fanaticism from such a captive audience in that South Carolina club let the members of Lifehouse—Jason Wade, Sergio Andrade, and Rick Woolstenhulme—know that they were on to something, that they had a genuine smash on their hands. "We almost didn't make it through the song 'cause our eyes were wide open," Jason would later recall to the Web site Launch.

It was with that wide-eyed attitude that Jason and his bandmates would embrace their fame. "Moment" announced the band's arrival and offered Lifehouse a future in pop music. But it also was the culmination of years of hard work. This book will examine Lifehouse's rise to fame: the humble beginnings performing for a youth-group audience, the highs and lows of its major-label record deal, and how the band members ultimately learned the importance of being true to themselves. By tracing the band's path, we'll see how Lifehouse achieved success.

Chapter One

In the Beginning

A lot happened before Lifehouse ruled the airwaves. The band's story starts during the childhood of Jason Wade, who isn't just the band's singer and guitarist—he's also Lifehouse's main writer. Lifehouse has a full, multi-instrumental sound, and Jason is generally considered its main creative force. He has written almost all of the band's music on guitar by himself, and he is the sole member who has stayed with the band throughout its duration. He's even called Lifehouse's sound "singer-songwriter rock," which emphasizes his big role in the band and the personal nature of his lyrics. Singer-songwriters are typically billed as solo acts, such as Bob Dylan and Jack Johnson. Lifehouse simply would not be Lifehouse without Jason.

Lifehouse's singer, guitarist, and songwriter, Jason Wade, performs in 2001, when the band toured to promote its debut album, *No Name Face*. As frontman, Jason could be considered the face of Lifehouse. He is the only member to have stayed in the band since it was founded.

Jason was born July 5, 1980, and spent his first five years in Camarillo, California, a town that's roughly midway between Santa Barbara and Los Angeles. When he was five years old, his family moved to Hawaii, where his parents were trained as Christian missionaries. Jason spent the next few years traveling with his parents to locations such as Japan, Thailand, Singapore, and Hong Kong. The experience was not ideal, as Jason and his family were considered outsiders and looked down upon by the native people, whom they attempted to convert to their religious beliefs. "They thought we were witches bringing trouble to their neighborhood," recalled Jason in a press release on Musicremedy.com. Though his parents' work involved attempting to convert people to Christianity, Jason says they took a more hands-off approach to raising him, encouraging him to draw his own conclusions about spirituality.

Around the time he was ten years old, Jason and his family returned to the United States, this time settling in Oregon. There, a home-schooled Jason began studying karate. He eventually earned a black belt. Though karate may not have much to do with music, it was one way that Jason learned how devoted he could be to a given interest. This attitude would prove unshakable and would eventually carry over to his music.

But first, Jason's creativity needed a boost. Unfortunately, this inspiration came by way of sadness. He began writing poems in the wake of his parents' divorce, which devastated him. Twelve-year-old Jason and his mother moved to the town of Port Orchard, Washington, near Seattle, in 1992 just as the area's own music scene, widely known as grunge, was becoming popular all over the country. Jason, however, wouldn't absorb the music by the likes of Nirvana and Pearl Jam until later in life. In fact, he has said that he didn't grow up listening to much popular music at all (though his mother did introduce him to the Beatles, who would prove to be a major inspiration). In those days, Jason mostly concentrated on writing words as a sort of therapy, and the pain he felt in the wake of his parents' divorce needed a major creative outlet.

One day, when he was about fifteen, Jason picked up a guitar of his mother's. She had been a storytelling folksinger who had toured the country years before as part of her scholarship to Pepperdine University in Malibu, California. Soon, Jason was teaching himself chords, inventing melodies, and setting his lyrics to music.

Banding Together

Jason's interest in music helped ease him into yet another transition he had to face: his move to Los Angeles. While he could turn to his guitar for solace in dealing with once again being the new kid on the block, music also helped him form a bond that would last for many years. His next-door neighbor was fellow music enthusiast Sergio Andrade. The two soon found that they had much in common. Born October 17, 1976, Sergio was also the son of missionaries. He and his family had moved from Guatemala to California when he was fourteen. Sergio also had a musician parent: his father played the keyboard. That set off Sergio's passion for playing music at an early age.

Jason and Sergio honed their songwriting craft by working together in their garages during extended jam sessions. With the

Original Lifehouse bassist Sergio Andrade plays with the band at a Chicago concert in 2003. Sergio, like frontman Jason Wade, comes from a musical family, and his training goes beyond the bass. Before joining Lifehouse, Sergio played keyboards, trombone, flute, and drums.

confidence gained through their collaboration, the pair hooked up with a drummer, John "Diff" Palmer, and began playing Friday nights at the auditorium of their nondenominational Christian church, Malibu Vineyard. The trio was dubbed Bliss (later, Blyss) and quickly built up a following over a two-year residency. "They had a really good P.A. system there, and we could do whatever we wanted," said Jason in a press release posted on VH1.com. "We got smoke machines and lights and basically turned it into this little club scene. Kids would come from all over, and we started filling the place up. At one point we were getting, like, 450 people out every week."

Blissful Existence

It was a fruitful time for the young band, though Bliss still had a lot of growing to do. By 1997, the band was playing not just in the Malibu Vineyard Church auditorium, but also at gigs for Pepperdine University and the University of Southern California—not bad for Lifehouse members who were about the same age as their college-age audience. Bliss also played a two-week stint touring colleges in Oklahoma. It was a great learning experience for the band that one day would become Lifehouse. "[We] went through a lot of phases trying to find our sounds," Sergio recalled later in a press release on Musicremedy.com. "We learned from our mistakes. We'd see tapes of ourselves onstage and go, 'This is horrible.' But we'd just say, 'OK, we gotta fix it,' and go back and practice some more."

The band's attention-grabbing residency at Malibu Vineyard Church led to the most important point in its prefame development: the recording of a demo. With the help of fellow Malibu Vineyard Church attendee and still-learning producer Ron Aniello, Bliss recorded *Diff's Lucky Day*, named for drummer John "Diff" Palmer's conversion to Christianity. The band pressed roughly 1,000 copies of *Diff's Lucky Day* (under both spellings of its name, Bliss and Blyss), which has since become something of a collector's item among Lifehouse fans. Today, original copies can fetch hundreds of dollars on eBay and other online outlets.

With a growing profile as a live act and the hard evidence of its skill on tape, it was only a matter of time before record labels came knocking. The band signed with the now-defunct DreamWorks Records, the main major label to show interest. "It was basically knowing the right people and getting our demos into the right people's hands that got us a record deal," Jason later told Pollstar.com, an online resource for concert information. "We didn't go through a bidding war. We knew DreamWorks was the one when we first started talking to them."

Before it could release anything, or even really start recording, the band had to make a major change: its name. Another band had already been performing and recording under the name Bliss. Jason and his bandmates came up with "Lifehouse," which they only later realized was also the name of a doomed rock opera that was to be released by Pete Townshend from the band The Who. It was a fateful coincidence, though, and in less than two years, "Lifehouse" became a known name.

Chapter Two

Putting the Life in Lifehouse

With a new deal and a new name, Lifehouse was on its way to stardom. The band entered the studio with Ron Aniello, the producer of the band's demo. Aside from his work on *Diff's Lucky Day*, Ron was a relative newcomer to the music scene who had never turned out a hit (though he would go on to craft successes for acts such as Days of the New and Jars of Clay). Also in the studio was Brendan O'Brien, a veteran mixer and engineer whose prior work included manning the boards for the Black Crowes, the Red Hot Chili Peppers, Aerosmith, Sheryl Crow, Stone Temple Pilots, and Pearl Jam. (Lifehouse has frequently been compared to these last two bands.) Brendan was such a whiz in the studio that he would mix about three of the band's recordings a day.

Sergio, onetime Lifehouse touring guitarist Stuart Mathis, Rick, and Jason *(from left)* perform at the My VH1 Music Awards in 2001. Though these musicians made up the band's 2001 touring lineup, Sergio and Jason were the only two members of this grouping to perform on Lifehouse's 2000 debut album.

The product of these sessions, *No Name Face*, was an album seeped in Jason's past. He has called it an album of self-discovery, and songs like "Somebody Else's Song" deal directly with that theme. Almost all of the album's twelve songs grapple with the emotional state that led up to the point of recording. "My songs come from a broken place," Jason told *People* magazine. "Writing was therapeutic for me."

Many of the cuts that made the album were originally included on *Diff's Lucky Day* and dated back at least five years, before the "official" demo was made. "Trying," for example, was five years old by the time it made it onto *No Name Face*. The only major difference between the songs' original recordings and the final album versions was the vocals—Jason had to rerecord them because his voice had changed over the course of the five years.

Though it deals with Jason's upbringing and challenges, *No Name Face* skirts a major part of his and the band's development: religion. Having emerged as part of a Christian youth group, Jason was careful to craft lyrics that were not explicitly about faith. "Songs can be interpreted in a million different ways, and that's my style of writing," Jason explained to MTV. "I like to ask a lot of questions and put half of it out there and let the audience figure out how to apply it to their own lives."

Still, it's hard to ignore the religious influence in the band's lyrics. "Everything," which originated during their Malibu Vineyard Church days, seems to speak directly to a higher power. "Breathing," another track from the band's pre-DreamWorks period, is even more explicit, with a mention of heaven.

Although the lyrics are laced with faith-based messages, the band has refrained from the preaching and worship typical of bands in the Christian rock sphere. Part of Lifehouse's mission has been to reach out to as many people as possible and not set religious boundaries. "My ultimate goal in writing songs is simply to connect with people," Jason said in a press release on VH1.com.

Though Jason handled most of *No Name Face*'s writing, Sergio had some input on the finished product. "Jason would usually have the song written before he'd bring it to us," he said in a press release on Musicremedy.com. "Then we all kind of arrange it together. The way we work on songs feels really natural, which I think has a lot to do with us being tight as a band and as friends."

Ron Aniello also had a hand in writing, but his largest role was in crafting the sound of the album. Jason was so excited upon entering a real recording studio for the first time that he wanted to make full use of it by layering sounds and special effects onto his band's simple guitar-rock template. Ron, however, discouraged such heavy production. The resulting stripped-down sound of *No Name Face* led to its being labeled postgrunge: a bit slicker than the grunge rock of the early 1990s, while still embracing the spirit of grunge with its hard-rock edge and emotional lyrics.

Time to Face the World

During the time between the completion of *No Name Face* in the summer of 2000 and its October 31, 2000, release date, the band hit the road for a tour. Before either the album's release or the tour, however, something happened that would become familiar for the band: a lineup change. During the recording of *No Name Face*, drummer John Palmer left Lifehouse. On the album, he was replaced by session drummer Matt Laug. Since Matt was strictly studio-based, John's departure meant the band needed a full-time drummer it could take on the road. That's when Rick Woolstenhulme signed on.

Rick, who was born September 20, 1979, shared a common bond with his bandmates—he, too, came from a musical family. His parents played piano, and his brother played guitar. From an early age, Rick was encouraged to play the drums. The Arizona native spent his early years playing in other bands, one of which shared rehearsal space with Lifehouse. When Rick heard that Lifehouse was looking for a drummer, he tried out and was chosen for the band.

Rick's entry into Lifehouse was smooth, and he formed a quick bond with his new bandmates. The seamless transition was important because soon after Rick became Lifehouse's drummer in 2000, the band received its biggest break yet: opening for Pearl Jam. Lifehouse toured with Pearl Jam in September and October, though its members weren't quite living a glamorous,

Rick drums at a Lifehouse show in 2005. Rick's love for the drums was fostered at an early age when his family bought him a drum kit. Before joining Lifehouse, Rick attended the Los Angeles Music Academy.

rock-star lifestyle. For one thing, Lifehouse did not play on the same stage as Pearl Jam. Lifehouse was relegated to a smaller side stage, which meant the band would often play to fewer than 400 people—a smaller crowd than even Bliss played for at its peak. "A lot of people would pass us by on the way to their seats," Jason said about the stint to the *Daily Bruin* newspaper. Additionally, no one in Lifehouse actually got to meet anyone in Pearl Jam. The band still had a long way to go before its members could rub elbows with rock heroes.

HOW LIFEHOUSE HELPED CHANGE POP MUSIC

When Lifehouse entered the realm of popular music in 2000, it offered something of an alternative to the music that was dominating the airwaves. On rock stations, heavy rap-rock bands like Limp Bizkit and Korn took up most of the slots. On pop or Top 40 stations, the teen-pop boom of the late 1990s that made stars out of 'N Sync, Britney Spears, the Backstreet Boys, and Christina Aguilera was still very much in effect.

With its catchy brand of melodic rock, Lifehouse enchanted both rock and pop radio formats. Along with other rockers with accessible music, such as Matchbox Twenty and Creed, Lifehouse helped change both types of stations. Lifehouse propped open the door of rock radio for bands with emotionally invested lyrics like Nickelback and The Killers. On the pop front, the influence of the band's mature rock sensibility could be heard even in teenybopper stars like Kelly Clarkson and Ashlee Simpson, who instead of basing their music in soul and R & B like many singers in the genre before them, choose more of a rock edge. As *Rolling Stone* put it in 2001, "The remarkable success of Lifehouse signals that the teen audience that's made stars of Britney [Spears] and Justin [Timberlake] is beginning to grow up."

Clearly, Lifehouse was no overnight sensation. While the band was on the road with Pearl Jam and then Better Than Ezra in 2000, something was happening on radio stations across the country: the power ballad "Hanging by a Moment" was beginning to take off. It first started with rock radio stations picking up the song and spinning it into heavy rotation. Then, Top 40 stations followed suit. By the time Lifehouse hit the road with Matchbox Twenty and Everclear in February 2001 for a one-month tour, "Hanging by a Moment" was everywhere. No one was more shocked at the song's success than Jason. "I just wrote that song without thinking of what was gonna happen to it and then it just kinda took over from there," he told Launch.

Jason later confessed that the song took about five minutes to write. That five-minute effort became the yearlong anthem of 2001. It topped Billboard's year-end Hot 100 chart, thanks to its longevity on playlists (it never reached the top spot of the weekly Hot 100, peaking at number 2). At the Billboard Awards in December, Lifehouse picked up two awards: Hot 100 Single of the Year and New Artist of the Year. A multiformat smash, "Hanging by a Moment" was the most-played song on radio in 2001.

Lifehouse was on top of the world. Unfortunately, the band did not know how tough fame would be.

Chapter Three

Hanging by a Thread

By April 2001, *No Name Face* had been certified platinum by the Recording Industry Association of America (it would go on to achieve double-platinum status). "Hanging by a Moment" was everywhere, and so was the band. Now with four members (touring guitarist Stuart Mathis had entered the fold), Lifehouse toured almost nonstop throughout 2001. The stint with Matchbox Twenty and Everclear gave way to a summer trek with 3 Doors Down and Tantric. Lifehouse rounded out fall with a headlining tour.

All the while, Lifehouse's live show was at odds with its album. *No Name Face* was full of pensive ballads and slow tunes that did not exactly have the juice to charge crowds.

Before Lifehouse performs, the band sits in silence for about half an hour as part of a preconcert ritual. After shows, its members usually take the time to meet fans and sign autographs. Here, Lifehouse performs in Uniondale, New York, in 2001.

While "Moment" was a crowd-pleasing anthem, the band had to reconfigure some of the songs on *No Name Face* to fit into the live format. "On the record, there's a couple of tracks that are more mellow, with acoustic guitars and stuff. But in our live show, we've been trying to keep it really up-tempo," Jason told MTV.com. "[Our live show has] gotten a lot rockier than on the record. We try to step it up with the guitars, getting them crunchier and picking the tempos up to draw the crowd in more."

Have a Little Faith

Lifehouse was also at odds with its own image and roots. Many Christian rock fans remembered the band from its days playing the Malibu Vineyard Church. With the increasing attention Lifehouse received in 2001, even people who weren't aware of the band back then could detect a religious undercurrent in its sound. From the start of their major-label career, Lifehouse members adamantly denied that the band made religious rock.

"I don't even like the word 'religion,'" Jason told *Rolling Stone*. "My music is spiritually based, but we don't want to be labeled a 'Christian band,' because all of a sudden, people's walls come up and they won't listen to your music and what you have to say."

Even more than that, Jason felt he could be inherently Christian without publicizing his beliefs. "A Christian plumber is just a plumber," he told the *Daily Bruin*. Still, Jason never refuted the importance of his spirituality, telling *CosmoGIRL!* in 2002 that "[it's] the biggest thing that keeps me grounded. It's the backbone to my music and a huge inspiration for my lyrics. It doesn't let all this go to my head, and it helps me realize there's

Jason is in the spotlight at this 2001 concert in Los Angeles, California. Lifehouse's frontman has a love-hate relationship with fame, which he says was never his goal for playing music.

a reason for it all. My spiritual background does leave a lot of my thoughts open for interpretation. I always leave things open so people can figure out what they want the song to be to them."

Coping with Fame

Besides its image, Lifehouse had yet another thing to come to terms with: overwhelming success. "Moment" was so popular for so long that it dwarfed everything else on *No Name Face*. The two other singles the band released to radio, "Breathing" and "Sick Cycle Carousel," failed to take off. Not even the wacky, eye-popping "Carousel" video could wrestle listeners away from "Moment." On one hand, this underscored the phenomenal success of "Moment," but it also indicated unfortunate things to come.

In early 2002, Lifehouse began recording its second album, *Stanley Climbfall*. Again, the band enlisted Ron Aniello to produce the set, which was created over the course of two months in a

JASON WADE'S SONGWRITING INFLUENCES

Though Jason Wade says he didn't grow up with much popular music around the house, he quickly absorbed the sounds of many who came before him, as well as a few of his peers. Here's a sampling of the artists who Jason has cited as helping him become the song-writer that he is today.

Chris Martin of Coldplay performs in 2005.

Paul McCartney
Cat Stevens
The Beach Boys
Nirvana
Elliott Smith
Rufus Wainwright
Radiohead
Coldplay

Hollywood studio. Brendan O'Brien, who mixed *No Name Face*, also mixed *Climbfall* in May in Atlanta, Georgia.

While *No Name Face* largely dealt with Jason's coming to terms with his past, *Climbfall* was about the present. "The main theme on this album captures the lyric in [the first single] 'Spin,' about not changing anything about your past and basically taking the good with the bad and realizing that you need both to be balanced and live a normal life," Jason told *Rolling Stone*.

Climbfall was also largely influenced by Lifehouse's experiences on the road. Jason aimed to write an upbeat album that would translate better in concert than the mostly mid-tempo and introspective *No Name Face*. Many of *Climbfall*'s tracks were played in concert before they were recorded, and Jason wrote the album during the 2001 tour, making demo recordings by using a four-track recorder he set up on the tour bus.

Almost fifty-five songs were written as possible candidates for the new album, and many of them reflected the music to which Jason had been listening. Early on, he characterized the album to MTV.com as "U2 meets Coldplay." Later, other British bands influenced the mix, including the innovative rock band Radiohead. "We wanted to make some of these songs more atmospheric," Jason told VH1.

At the start of 2001, Lifehouse spent almost a year and a half on the road in the wake of its debut album, touring with the likes of Everclear, 3 Doors Down, and Tantric. Lifehouse itself headlined a series of shows. A lot of *Stanley Climbfall*'s material was written while on tour and audience-tested before the album's release.

While Jason and Ron again took a less-is-more approach to the production, resulting in a mostly raw sound, experimentation abounded on *Climbfall*. "My Precious" was written and recorded in the same day and exhibits the spontaneity of a jam session. Jason calls the title track "the most creative song" the band has ever recorded. He came up with the lyrics in an unconventional way: he mumbled, Ron wrote down what he thought Jason was saying, and soon they had a song. "The Sky Is Falling" attempted to break out of the handful of chords that dominate popular modern rock. "[The song "Sky"] definitely has some changes that I found that I didn't even know about on the first record," Jason told *Rolling Stone* on his growing sophistication as a songwriter.

The first single, "Spin," was a back-to-basics effort—and not just in sound. Jason originally wrote the song when he was thirteen, in the wake of his parents' divorce. Still, the track's function as a "positive, uplifting song about moving on," as Jason explained it to TeenPeople.com, fit well with *Climbfall*'s theme.

A Moment Passed

Moving on is just what Lifehouse did. In the months leading up to *Climbfall*'s September 17, 2002, release, the band embarked on yet another tour. This time, it enlisted Sean Woolstenhulme,

Rick's brother, to play lead guitar on the road. Sean, however, was no stranger to touring with the band. The year before, his band, the Calling, opened for Lifehouse.

Lifehouse hit Europe for a trek and then returned to the United States in November to open for the Rolling Stones. The experience was much different from its early days opening for Pearl Jam. The Rolling Stones met Lifehouse and showed support for the much younger band. Jason called the stint the highlight of Lifehouse's touring career up to that point.

Time on the road also allowed the band to see the effect of its music on fans firsthand. Lifehouse, which to this day will spend up to an hour and a half meeting fans and signing autographs after concerts, has always emphasized on making such direct connections. "Having a certain amount of fans connect with the first record really kind of validates what you're doing," Jason explained to *Rolling Stone*. "It really makes you feel like you're doing it for a reason. I'm 50/50 on [fame]. I love the fact that people are connecting to the lyrics, but performing live and photo shoots and that kind of stuff is my least favorite part of all this. Who wants people to just stare at you and analyze you all day long? That can be kind of difficult, especially because I never did this to become a rock star or a famous person or whatever.

I just chose a couple of friends to get out of my room and actually play these songs, but it's something that I have to deal with."

However fulfilling reaching many people could be, *Climbfall* did not live up to expectations. The singles "Spin" and "Take Me Away" failed to make the mark on radio that "Hanging by a Moment" had the previous year. Though *Climbfall* debuted in the Top 10 of the Billboard 200, it quickly fell off the charts and failed to attain gold status.

Even worse, as part of the music-label mergers that dominated the early 2000s, Lifehouse's record label, DreamWorks, was bought by Universal Music Group. Because *Climbfall* fared so poorly on the charts, the band was dropped and found itself without a record deal for almost six months in 2003. With the days of climbing the charts seemingly in the past, Lifehouse looked to be in a freefall.

Chapter Four

Nothing Else to Lose

If the commercial failure of Lifehouse's second album, *Stanley Climbfall*, came as a surprise at first, the band quickly realized why. Jason would later blame the sophomore slump on the staying power of "Moment" and *Climbfall*'s harder-to-digest vibe. "We were definitely trying to make this creative rock record that I don't think anyone really wanted to hear," he told SheKnows.com. It wasn't just the continued airplay of "Moment" that took a toll on Lifehouse; it was the band's popularity in general. Jason said that during the writing of *Climbfall*, he felt pressure to live up to the hype, to play to the expectations of his crowd. The album's demise, then, was a matter of Jason being less than true to himself in his writing.

Rick *(left)* and Jason arrive at a Matchbox Twenty DVD release party in 2004. The pair reunited after taking time off after Lifehouse's disastrous second album, *Stanley Climbfall.* The sessions for the band's third album produced more than fifty songs.

With no record deal and a recently flopped album, times were hard for Lifehouse. "It almost felt like it was kind of over," Jason later told andPOP.com. He contemplated a solo career, Rick began looking for other gigs, and Sergio Andrade, Lifehouse's bassist from when the band was called Bliss, quietly departed. It seemed the band was doomed.

Hope, though, came in 2004 when Universal's Geffen Records decided to pick up Lifehouse for more albums. The new deal inspired Jason and Rick—the only remaining members—to begin work again. "We realized how much we missed being on the road and how much we loved what we do," Jason told andPOP. "I thought we should just go for it and see where we could take it."

The first order of business was to replace Sergio. Jason and Rick held a "cattle call" audition, seeing as many bass players as they could in as short a time as possible, but they could not find anyone they thought would fit in the band. Then, Rick's brother, Sean, who had toured as a guitarist with Lifehouse, recommended Bryce Soderberg, a Canada native who had been playing in the guitar-pop band AM Radio. Bryce immediately formed a musical and personal rapport with Jason and Rick. With three members again, it was time to record.

Never Seemed So Alive

Instead of holing up in a lavish stand-alone studio, Lifehouse recorded its self-titled third album in the home studio of producer John Alagia. John had previously worked with the likes of the Dave Matthews Band, O.A.R., and John Mayer. Since John owned the recording space, Lifehouse did not feel the pressure that bands often feel when they must produce music within the limited studio time for which they paid.

The relaxed approach to recording could be heard in the third album. Working for the first time with John Alagia did not prove to be a challenge, as he stuck to Ron Aniello's goal of creating

Bryce Soderberg became Lifehouse's full-time bassist in 2004, taking over from Sergio Andrade, the band's founding bassist. Bryce grew up in Canada and moved to Los Angeles in 2000 to attend the Musicians Institute, where members of the Red Hot Chili Peppers and Weezer also studied.

a rock sound that is as basic as possible. Rick described the album to Umusic as "fat and full, but . . . not cluttered."

Lifehouse, however, wasn't as hard-edged or up-tempo as *Stanley Climbfall*—it was similar to the more introspective and mid-tempo *No Name Face*. "This record really reminds me of the first one, because on the first record I had no pretense, I had no fan base, I never had a song on the radio," Jason told SheKnows.com. "So I didn't have all that pressure of where it's

Lifehouse plays a show in Atlanta, Georgia, in May 2005. The group's current members have commented on their connection. "It feels like I'm fifteen again," says Jason in the band's press release for its self-titled third album. "The three of us hang out all the time, play basketball, and go out to eat. It feels right."

going to fit in—I could just kind of be creative and just make all my music, and then hopefully people would respond to it . . . That seems to be the best formula for us."

Free from the pressure to create a hit, Lifehouse did what felt natural: Jason and his bandmates simply let themselves be themselves. That's part of the explanation for the album title. *Lifehouse* is meant to be a picture of the band at the time of its creation. Jason said the title also has to do with the tumultuous time the band went through before the album's release—the lineup and label changes made its members feel like they were finally starting anew.

New Lease on Life

Lifehouse quietly made its way into stores on March 22, 2005. A few weeks later, the album bowed at number 10 on the Billboard 200 chart—not bad for a group that many considered to be washed-up. The band further continued its slow climb back to the top with the set's first single, the ballad "You and Me," which Rick called "the wedding song of the year." Released in early 2005, the single took twenty-six weeks after its debut to hit the Top 10 on the Billboard Hot 100. Both it and the album were certified gold, and the single peaked at an impressive number 5.

"I think we might have shied away from releasing a ballad a few years ago, but part of this whole rebirth for us has been trying not to over-think anything," Jason told MTV.com. "To write love songs that people connect to is not a bad thing."

Connecting with people was nothing new for Lifehouse, though. The band spent almost the entirety of 2005 on the road, promoting its third album via talk-show appearances and a steady stream of concerts. In September, Lifehouse perhaps became more accessible than ever, stripping down its sound for the *Live*

Session EP, a four-song "live" set recorded in the studio and released on the iTunes Music Store. It features exclusive versions of two songs from *No Name Face* ("Hanging by a Moment" and "Breathing") and two *Lifehouse* tracks ("You and Me" and "All in All").

In just five years, Lifehouse had come full circle: from the astonishing success of its first single to its overlooked second album to its eponymous comeback set. Through behind-the-scenes changes and navigating the fickle waters of pop music, Jason Wade rediscovered his band's center by looking inside himself and choosing to express his truth. As he told MTV, "When you're finally comfortable in your own skin, and comfortable with what you do, then you can't help but do it the best you can."

Timeline

1996 Bliss forms and begins playing at the Malibu Vineyard Church.

1998 Bliss records its demo *Diff's Lucky Day*.

1999 Bliss signs with DreamWorks Records and changes its name to Lifehouse.

2000 Lifehouse begins touring North America and ends up staying on the road for eighteen more months. Drummer John Palmer leaves the band. Lifehouse releases its debut album, *No Name Face*.

2001 "Hanging by a Moment" is named the number 1 single of the year by *Billboard*.

2002 Lifehouse releases its second album, *Stanley Climbfall*.

2003 DreamWorks is bought out; Lifehouse is without a label.

2004 Sergio Andrade, a founding member of Bliss, leaves Lifehouse. Lifehouse signs with Geffen Records. Bryce Soderberg joins Lifehouse as its new bassist.

2005 Lifehouse releases its third album, *Lifehouse*. Lifehouse returns to the Top 10 of the Billboard Hot 100 with "You and Me."

Discography

1998 *Diff's Lucky Day* (self-released)
2000 *No Name Face* (DreamWorks)
2002 *Stanley Climbfall* (DreamWorks)
2005 *Lifehouse* (Geffen)
2005 *Live Session* EP (Geffen; iTunes exclusive)

Glossary

bidding war A situation in which multiple record labels are all trying to sign the same band. A label might attempt to one-up the others by offering the band more money than the rest are offering.

demo A tape or CD featuring rough, unpolished recordings. Artists, particularly those who aren't signed to record labels, use demos to drum up interest in their music by sending them to prospective employers.

eponymous Relating to a person for whom someone or something, such as an album, is named; self-titled.

four-track A primitive, low-fidelity recording device that allows four channels of sound (for example, one for guitar, one for vocals, one for drums, and one for bass). Four-tracks were often used to record demos.

gold In terms of recorded music, this signifies the shipment of 500,000 copies of a record, as certified by the Recording Industry Association of America (RIAA). This is used as an indicator of how many copies the album has sold.

heavy rotation Frequent airplay for a song on the radio.

jam A loose, spontaneous musical performance.

platinum Used to describe the shipment of one million copies of a recorded release, as certified by the RIAA. Records that sell two million copies are labeled double platinum, three million in sales is called triple platinum, and so on.

pop Short for "popular," and often describes music that is well liked, regardless of genre. Pop music is particularly melodic and catchy.

rap-rock A type of music that thrived in the late 1990s and early 2000s. It featured rapped vocals, but a guitar-based, hard-rock sound. Bands like Korn and Limp Bizkit helped popularize this style.

residency A regular gig performed for a period of time in the same venue.

session drummer A professional drummer who typically plays on bands' albums, but is not officially part of that band. A session musician is often employed by a studio and will appear on many of that studio's releases.

sophomore slump A somewhat legendary, dreaded "curse" in music that occurs when an artist or band's second album fails to live up to the expectations set by its successful first album.

For More Information

MTV Networks
1515 Broadway
New York, NY 10036
(212) 258-8000
http://www.mtv.com

Relevant magazine
100 South Lake Destiny Drive,
   Suite 200
Orlando, FL 32810
(407) 660-1411
Web site: http://www.
   relevantmagazine.com

Web Sites

Due to the changing nature of
Internet links, the Rosen
Publishing Group, Inc., has
developed an online list of
Web sites related to the subject
of this book. This site is
updated regularly. Please use
this link to access the list:

http://www.rosenlinks.com/
   cmtm/life

For Further Reading

Alfonso, Barry. *The Billboard Guide to Contemporary Christian Music*. New York, NY: Billboard Books, 2002.

George-Warren, Holly, Patricia Romanowski, and Jon Pareles. *The Rolling Stone Encyclopedia of Rock and Roll*. New York, NY: Fireside, 2001.

Joseph, Mark. *Faith, God and Rock 'n' Roll*. London, England: Sanctuary Publishing, 2003.

Leikin, Molly-Ann. *How to Write a Hit Song: The Complete Guide to Writing and Marketing Chart-Topping Lyrics and Music*. Milwaukee, WI: Hal Leonard Corporation, 1989.

Lifehouse. *No Name Face (Play-It-Like-It-Is)*. New York, NY: Cherry Lane Music, 2001.

Bibliography

Bottemly, C. "The Second Coming of Lifehouse." August 8, 2002. Retrieved July 13, 2005 (http://www.vh1.com/artists/news/1457720/08052002/lifehouse.jhtml).

Brown, Lauren. "CosmoGIRL! Grooves with . . . Lifehouse's Jason Wade." *CosmoGIRL!*, Vol. 4, No. 8, October 2002, p. 146.

Charaipotra, Sona. "Spotlight on . . . Lifehouse." *People*, Vol. 56, No. 7, p. 40.

Davis, Darren. "Lifehouse Goes Platinum." April 4, 2001. Retrieved June 10, 2005 (http://launch.yahoo.com/read/news/12038391).

Devenish, Colin. "New Life for Lifehouse." September 17, 2002. Retrieved July 17, 2005 (http://www.rollingstone.com/news/story/5933548/new_life_for_lifehouse).

Gonshor, Adam. "Back with Third Album, Lifehouse Almost Split After Sophomore Bomb." March 9, 2005. Retrieved June 10, 2005 (http://www.andpop.com/article/4021).

"Lifehouse." August 6, 2001. Retrieved July 1, 2005 (http://www.pollstar.com/news/viewhotstar.pl?Artist=LIFEHO).

"Lifehouse Biography." 2000. Retrieved June 10, 2005 (Reprinted on http://www.vh1.com/artists/spotlight/inside_track/lifehouse/bio.jhtml and http://www.musicremedy.com/articles/51).

Montgomery, James. "Aided by John Mayer's Producer, Lifehouse Rebound from Sophomore Jinx." March 31, 2005. Retrieved June 10, 2005 (http://www.mtv.com/news/articles/1499343/20050331/index.jhtml?headlines=true).

Moriates, Chris. "Lifehouse Takes Life on the Road to Promote New Album." Nov. 21, 2000. Retrieved June 10, 2005 (http://www.dailybruin.ucla.edu/news/printable.asp?id=2075&date=11/21/2000).

Price, Nancy J. "10 Questions with Lifehouse." 2005. Retrieved August 1, 2005 (http://sheknows.com/about/look/6245.htm).

Shulz, Cara Lynn. "Know the Words: Lifehouse 'Spin.'" 2002. Retrieved July 13, 2005 (http://www.teenpeople.com/teenpeople/2002/stars/words/100402_lifehouse.html).

Umusic. "Lifehouse." 2005. Retrieved June 10, 2005 (http://umusic.ca/lifehouse).

Weiss, Neal, and Jason Gelman. "Lifehouse's 'Hanging' a Highlight of 2001." December 14, 2001. Retrieved June 10, 2005 (http://launch.yahoo.com/read/news/12049162).

Wild, David. "The Rock and Roll Gospel According to Lifehouse." *Rolling Stone*, No. 870, June 7, 2001, pp. 45–46.

Index

About the Author

Rich Juzwiak lives in Brooklyn, New York, where he writes about music for various publications and rants about everything on his blog, fourfour.

Photo Credits

Designer: Gene Mollica; **Editor:** Jun Lim
Photo Researcher: Gene Mollica